THE EXTREMELY SERIOUS
GUIDE TO
MOVING HOUSE

THE EXTREMELY SERIOUS GUIDE TO MOVING HOUSE

KEITH RAY

COLUMBUS BOOKS
LONDON

Copyright © 1987 Keith Ray
First published in Great Britain in 1987 by
Columbus Books Limited
19-23 Ludgate Hill, London EC4M 7PD

Designed by Kirby-Sessions, London
Typeset by Falcon Graphic Art Ltd
Wallington, Surrey
Printed and bound by R.J. Acford Ltd
Chichester, Sussex

ISBN 0 86287 346 0

CONTENTS

Introduction   7

Reasons for Moving House   11
Symptoms of the Urge Coming On   13
Ways of Suppressing the House-Moving Urge   15
Are You Fit Enough to Move House?   16
Are You Emotionally and Psychologically Suited to Moving House?   19
On Being Rational about Moving House   22
When to Move House   23

The Ideal House   25
Estate Agents' Details   28
House Photographs   39
Real Danger Signs   41

Choosing a Solicitor   43
Understanding Solicitors   46
The Campaign for Real Conveyancing   49

Surveyors' Reports   51
Choosing a Removal Firm   54

Applying for a Loan   58
Whom to Go to for a Loan   60
How Much Will You Be Able to Borrow?   65

Choosing an Estate Agent   67
Sale Details for Your Own House   73
Types of Viewer   75
Ways of Discouraging Potential Buyers You Don't Like   77

How to Sell Your House Yourself   79
Addresses   81

Technical Problems with Moving House   83
The Cost of Moving House   85

Moving House and Sex   88

Frequency of Moving House   91
A Final Word   95

'*Well, the kids seem to be settling in pretty well.*'

INTRODUCTION

We must have been crazy, totally crazy. Having sworn blind we'd never, ever, repeat the experience – not in a million years – there we were doing it yet again: moving house. Some deep-rooted masochism seemed to be emerging for its five-yearly airing. There we were once more, going the rounds of estate agents, surveyors, estate agents, solicitors, estate agents, building societies, estate agents, removal firms, estate agents, estate agents and estate agents. Suddenly we were spending half our life showing total strangers without the remotest intention of buying round our immaculate house in their muddy shoes (prospective purchasers always seem to have muddy shoes; even after twelve weeks of continuous drought, with the landscape like parched sandpaper, wildlife gasping for breath and water on ration, you still get potential 'buyers' wearing wet, muddy shoes).

Now that was the root of the problem. Our house was immaculate. It was in perfect decorative condition and had not the slightest hint of structural disorder or weakness. And it was just the size we wanted, with charming neighbours, in a pleasant location close to schools, shops and work and yet idyllically quiet, it had beautiful gardens and a fantastic view. It was ideal for our needs. We loved that house . . . yet we were about to abandon it and move.

We couldn't for the life of us remember why, but there we were on the brink of leaving our dream home to move to a house that was far too big for us, grossly over-priced, miles from anywhere, practically falling down and rotting away (what estate agents describe as 'in immaculate decorative order'), over-run by various species of rodent, with a jungle of a garden, and so heavily mortgaged that even paying for the next meal looked like an impossible financial high-wire act. Moving house seemed to have a fatal fascination for us, in the same way that moths are mortally attracted to a naked bulb or wasps to a sticky jam jar. Some people dice with death sky-diving or hang-gliding; others risk life and limb motor-racing; still others experiment with hard drugs, or enter the exciting world of crime . . . but what do *we* do for kicks? We move house!

Four months of absolute hell, two gazumpings, four broken 'chains', three lost contracts, five threats of divorce and 698 flaming rows later, we moved into our new home (well, not so much 'into' as on top of, since the whole place was crammed full of junk). In fact the only thing 'new' about this residence was the range of headaches and worries it provided us with. In terms of the civilized development of our lives, we suddenly took a backward step of approximately 25 years.

At that point we vowed that *this* time we'd never ever do it again . . . not in a billion years (at that stage, if I'd suddenly discovered the part of the brain responsible for the desire to move house I'd have begged a sympathetic brain surgeon to remove it). As a way of cementing our resolve we decided we'd write a book about the experience to warn other potential house-movers of the dangers. The only drawback might be if the book were so successful that we'd have to move to a bigger and more expensive house.

That, briefly, is how this book came about. Funnily enough, now that it's finished, we've just seen a rather nice little property round the corner from where we used to live . . . late Regency, with a really fine conservatory and the most delightful garden you could possibly imagine . . . and it's going for a song, considering its potential. Perhaps a quick viewing wouldn't do any real harm . . . we'd only have a look. After all, we resolved we'd never *really* move again, not in a billion years . . .

'*So you're the new owner of no. 12 . . . You* are *brave.*'

GOVERNMENT HEALTH WARNING

Moving house can seriously damage your health, wealth, marriage, sex life, career prospects, intellectual powers, enjoyment of life, appetite and sense of humour. Why not stick to something safer, like DIY, having a brain transplant or swimming the Atlantic blindfolded?

'*You must be our new neighbour . . . Make too much noise and I'll break yer legs.*'

REASONS FOR MOVING HOUSE

Most people who move house have some good reason for doing so. A reason is not essential, of course, but it certainly helps when, at the end of the fateful day, you sit amongst the chaos and ask yourself, 'Why did we do it?' If you have a valid reason it saves you the embarrassment of lying to yourself or pretending you didn't hear the question. By contrast, estate agents see such reasons as quite unnecessary handicaps to their earning more commission, and would prefer to see people moving weekly or even daily purely on a passing whim. Reasons are basically of two types: reasons why you *want* to move (e.g. you live next door to your mother-in-law) and reasons why you *have* to move (e.g. your house has fallen down). Some of the more common (and less common) reasons mentioned to estate agents include:

- to move to a bigger house;

- to move to a better or smarter house;

- to move to a more pleasant, quieter or classier neighbourhood;

- to move closer to your job;

- because the neighbours found out about you;

- to move further away from your mother-in-law, the taxman, debt collector, local fuzz, etc. (especially if they are all the same person);

- to move nearer to God by moving from, say, a bungalow to a three-storey town house;

- to spend a lot of surplus money (there are few things as effective for spending surplus and non-surplus money as moving house);

- to lose weight by moving to an area with a lower gravitational field (note, this will not reduce your mass or shape: you will merely feel lighter);

- to avoid decorating: in practice this is a fairly short-term viewpoint;

- to avoid cutting the lawn by moving to a house where the grass is shorter: generally speaking this is an even shorter-term reason;

- to avoid doing the washing-up by leaving all your dirty crockery and cutlery in your old house for the new occupier to deal with: this is one of the most short-sighted reasons for moving;

- to avoid changing TV channel by moving to a house where the television is already tuned to the channel you want and is included as part of the deal (possibly the most short-sighted reason of all for moving);

- for a pleasant change of oxygen molecules on the grounds that you've breathed every molecule in your existing house at least one hundred times over and are now beginning to recognize each one as an individual;

- to help avert poverty and hunger amongst estate agents, surveyors and conveyancers;

- because you get an erotic kick out of paying stamp duty (perhaps because the word 'stamp' appeals to some subconscious masochistic or sadistic tendency);

- to avoid returning your neighbours' invitation for drinks;

- to propel your metaphysical psyche into new dimensions of terrestrial existentialism (although absolute crap, this might sound impressive when you come to apply for an outsize mortgage);

- to avoid propelling your metaphysical psyche into new dimensions of terrestrial existentialism (this is a good reason for people who disagree with the logic behind the last reason);

- to improve your sex life (in fact, if you have to resort to moving house to improve your sex life, things must be pretty bad – in which case moving house is unlikely to make them worse);

- to ruin your sex life totally: moving house can leave you with so little spare time and energy that a sex life becomes a purely theoretical concept;

- to move to an area where the alignment of the Earth's magnetic field is more conducive to regular bowel habits (again, this is absolute rubbish, but it should provoke some interesting conversation in the local pub and provide a short cut to getting known by the locals, who might thereafter refer to you as 'that cack-brained weirdo');

- penis-envy (this is what psychiatrists would like to think controls practically everything we do: in house-removal terms this presumably means moving to a house where the neighbours have small penises or no penises at all – a fact not normally recorded on house details).

SYMPTOMS OF THE URGE TO MOVE COMING ON

Anyone who has become aware of the cost and life-threatening stress of moving house will probably appreciate a few simple guidelines for predicting the onset of a house-moving urge. Some of the critical signs are outlined below:

- your wife starts lingering outside estate agents' windows;

- you begin to notice that your friends are moving;

- your friends start to refer to your house as 'quaint';

- the tree you so clearly remember planting as a tiny sapling has to be cut down because it is now threatening the foundations;

- there's no more wall space left for pictures;

- your wife says she could do with a room for ironing;

- you can't land your helicopter in the garden;

- you've redecorated so many times some of the walls meet in the middle;

- when you give a dinner party you have to omit yourself from the guest list because there isn't enough room;

- you've run out of new companies to refit your kitchen;

- you've double-glazed the double glazing for the second time;

- in order to do any further improvements to your house, you have to blow bits of it up first;

- the taxman writes you a nice letter thanking you for not claiming very much tax relief on your mortgage, and asks you to check that it wasn't a simple typing error;

- the extension's extension's extension has just been extended;

- in order to do some more cavity wall insulation you've had to pay a builder to create cavities in previously solid walls;

- you've just finished cavity-insulating the double glazing;

- at least one room in the house is more than half full of cardboard boxes;

- you feel your wine cellar is too small – mainly because you haven't got one;

- you feel you ought to be a three-TV house but don't have three different rooms to put them in;

- you have to go on a diet in order to get into your sitting room;

- your footprints are worn into the floorboards;

- the local burglars know your habits so well they can break in and rob you whenever you sneeze, or even when you blink;

- you've lived in the same place so long that you yourself have been listed as a monument of historical interest.

WAYS OF SUPPRESSING THE HOUSE-MOVING URGE

Once it gets a grip on you, the house-moving urge is one of the strongest forces experienced by the human race, at least on a par with the urge for food, sex, physical safety and a good, interference-free television picture. And once it affects the female of the species it is virtually unstoppable. Amongst the few ways of minimizing the strength of the urge are the following:

- nail yourself to the floor;

- nail yourself to the roof (even more effective, since even when nailed to the floor you can accomplish all tasks related to house purchase short of actually moving in);

- keep reminding yourself how much it cost the last time, and how inflation will have made the cost even more extortionate;

- wear a T-shirt which says 'My mother-in-law will be able to come and stay every weekend once we've moved', just to remind yourself of the negative aspects;

- keep one piece of furniture damaged in the last move constantly on display in the most prominent position in the house;

- always spend all the money you earn so that none can ever accumulate to pay for the cost of moving;

- be so unpleasant to bank managers, building society managers and all other sources of finance that no one will ever give you a mortgage;

- marry a qualified surveyor: this will ensure that every house you look at will turn out to have serious structural faults;

- take a course of hypnotherapy to instil a subconscious aversion to house purchase;

- have a frontal, side and rear lobotomy to remove all traces of brain function related to contract-signing;

- petition your MP, or even better your Euro MP (if you know who he is – and few do), to have house removal made a felony;

- brick up all the windows in your current house, paint the whole thing lime green and flood all the ground-floor rooms in old diesel oil: whilst this may make life marginally less comfortable for you, it should effectively ensure that no one else will ever buy your house, hence stopping you from moving elsewhere.

ARE YOU FIT ENOUGH TO MOVE HOUSE?

'Next time get professionals to shift the really heavy stuff.'

Moving house puts a considerable strain on the human constitution, so before embarking on such an activity it is a good idea to make sure you are physically and psychologically up to it. The following simple tests should allow you to assess your personal suitability for moving. Try each test in turn; if you fail on any one of the tests you should think twice about leaving your present home.

Physical strength and stamina Moving house requires considerable reserves of both sheer brute strength and stamina. To see whether you possess the right qualities you will need:

- one heavy old wardrobe;
- a complete dinner service for 12 people;
- a roll of carpet at least 12 x 20 feet;
- a telephone;
- a lively dog;
- a bucketful of mud;
- three hungry children under the age of four;
- a notepad and pen;
- equipment for making tea;
- four friends pretending to be removal men;
- a display cabinet full of eighteenth-century Venetian glass.

First, load the dinner service into the wardrobe and place the wardrobe under your left arm. With the right arm, pour the mud over the dog and, whilst the hungry children charge around looking for food, simultaneously unroll and fit the carpet, instruct the 'removal men' on how to wrap up the glassware, feed the children, telephone your solicitor, make tea for everyone and write a letter to the estate agent. If you can succeed in doing all this without any of the china or glass getting broken, and without the dog leaving a speck of mud on the carpet, you should be able to cope with moving house.

Dealing with problems During the move itself a thousand and one problems can arise, ranging from the trivial (such as communal insanity) to the more complex (finding the house doesn't exist, for example, except as a photo in the estate agent's window). If you are unprepared or unfit for dealing with such difficulties, there is a real risk that you might find moving too much of a strain. As a dummy run for the big day itself, arrange for the following events to happen all within the space of one hour:

- the gas man calls round to investigate a leak;
- the electricity man calls round to read the meter;
- the budgie escapes;
- your 4-year-old has an acute attack of diarrhoea and trips over, cutting his leg open;
- the freezer goes on the blink and threatens to ruin £200 worth of food;
- your brother/sister and family drop in unexpectedly from Australia, announcing they intend to stay a week;
- you get made redundant;
- your solicitor phones up to say he has completed all the paperwork, but for the wrong house;
- a 40-ton block of concrete falls on your car, totally flattening it;
- the water tank in the roof springs a leak;
- you receive notice that a new motorway is about to be built through the garden of your new house;
- the mortgage rate rises to 75 per cent;
- tax relief on mortgage repayments is abolished;
- stamp duty is increased to 5000 per cent;
- you suffer a major cardiac infarction (a lovely word that simply means a blood clot in the heart, if that can ever be called simple).

If this combination of events causes you the slightest distress – if even the smallest area of sweat breaks in your armpits – then it is unlikely you could ever successfully survive the trauma of moving.

Disorientation   One of the most disturbing things about moving is the degree of disorientation you experience in a new house. You can assess whether this might have an undue effect on you in the following way:

- switch off the electricity to the house;
- move all the furniture from the bedrooms and pile it up on the landing so that the route from your bedroom to the bathroom involves climbing over or squeezing round at least three beds, two wardrobes, six chairs and three trunks;
- approximately half an hour before bedtime consume eight pints of strong beer;
- retire to bed blindfolded, and with both legs down the same leg of your pyjamas.

Then see whether, when a desperate call of nature wakes you up with a start, you can make the vital journey to the bathroom in total darkness before you wet yourself. If you fail, it might be safer to stay in your present house (or give up beer).

Poverty   Moving house will probably put a greater strain on your pocket than anything else (I have yet to meet the person who over-estimated the cost of moving). Testing out whether you have that essential hermit quality not to be affected by the material deprivation is really quite simple; if you can live on, and support a family on, a total net income not exceeding 25p per week for at least a year, then it is likely that the financial strain should leave few permanent marks. If you can't, then why not try appreciating the good points of your present abode?

ARE YOU EMOTIONALLY AND PSYCHOLOGICALLY SUITED TO MOVING HOUSE?

'It's a sad case, this one . . . he enjoys moving house.'

Many of the problems that arise when people attempt to move house stem from a basic emotional or psychological unsuitability for such activity. In order to see whether you are suitable or not, simply answer an honest 'yes' or 'no' to the questions below. If you score one 'yes' or more you are probably emotionally or psychologically incompatible with house-moving, and should consider instead undertaking something less stressful, such as free-fall parachute jumping or deposing South American governments.

- Do you get excessively niggled by little annoyances such as finding the house you are in the process of buying doesn't really exist, or is in the wrong town, or has no windows?

- Do trivial little mistakes sometimes irritate you (for example, solicitors losing contracts in the post, or building societies putting the wrong year on your mortgage approval)?

- Do you worry a lot about minor inconveniences (such as having nowhere to live next week, or the news that a motorway flyover is to be built over your new house)?

- Are the pressures of life sometimes too much for you (for example, completing mortgage application forms, arranging for a survey, seeing solicitors, raising bridging finance and paying off all your old telephone, gas, electricity, water and rate bills – all within one hour)?

- Are you easily upset by other people for no real reason (for example, finding that the vendors of your new house have agreed the sale with five different people)?

- Do you have difficulty controlling your emotions (for example, do you feel inclined to hit people for no good reason other than the fact that they are the third lot to have gazumped you in the space of one week)?

- Are you excessively attached to material things (for instance, would you worry if your piano were to lose a leg, or your dining table were to arrive at your new house in kit form)?

- Do you ever feel people are conspiring against you (for example, do you ever suspect that estate agents, solicitors and surveyors are only after your money)?

- Do you tend to have unrealistically high expectations (for example, that you can really move in on the agreed date)?

- Do you have a distorted view of reality (for instance, have you ever actually believed an estate agent)?

- Are you a perfectionist (for instance, do you expect to feel warm and secure in your new house, and do you assume it will have floors, ceilings, a water supply and drainage of some sort)?

- Do you worry about the future (whether, for example, you will ever be able to sell the house again, or whether it will remain standing for more than one week)?

- Do you worry about money (for example, how you will ever afford to pay the mortgage, rates or heating bills)?

- Do you get obsessive about detail and fail to see the real issues (for example, do you fail to notice how attractive the house is, but ponder instead on the subsidence, dry rot, lethal wiring, leaking roof, dampness, etc.)?

'That's right!!! Go and involve our new neighbours in your silly little row!'

ON BEING RATIONAL ABOUT MOVING HOUSE

(This page has been left intentionally blank. Moving house and being rational are totally incompatible activities.)

WHEN TO MOVE HOUSE

Almost everybody dreams of moving in the spring, so that they can enjoy summer in their new house putting everything in order at their leisure. In practice many people end up moving in mid-winter, when they can do virtually nothing in their new home except wait for burst pipes and frost damage to the roof. The real problem is that whatever month you would like to move in, there are usually good reasons why you can't. For example:

- **January**: this is no good because it's just after Christmas, so most people will be too broke to put in a decent offer on your current house. Also most people have hangovers, and decide to wait for spring.

- **February**: far too cold to move. Most solicitors, surveyors and removal men are sunning it in the Bahamas on the proceeds of last year's killings.

- **March**: too wet and miserable to move. The removal firms advise against having all your furniture out in the damp. Also most prospective buyers are too busy thinking about their summer holidays.

- **April**: a good time to move from the weather standpoint, but it also marks the start of the spring price increases, so although you may be able to sell your own place, anything *you* fancy will probably have leapt out of your reach.

- **May**: an ideal time to move, but it's peak mortgage-demand period, and you can't raise the finance for love or money.

- **June**: this is when everyone wants to move, and if you haven't booked a year ahead you'll never get a removal firm with which you could risk your household effects.

- **July**: just as you get the mortgage offer you suddenly find that all prospective buyers are starting to disappear for their holidays. The estate agent says it might be better to wait a month.

- **August**: peak holiday month, and probably too hot to move. Building societies start to run short of cash because everyone has been withdrawing their savings for their holidays.

- **September**: just as prospective buyers start to show interest, you find that your solicitor is taking a late holiday (to avoid all the riff-raff house buyers, of course) and takes so long to get anything moving that your potential buyer loses interest. Building societies are still short of money after holiday withdrawals.

- **October**: quite a good time really: your solicitor is back from the sun, you've got a mortgage offer, the weather is great for moving . . . but in order to move now you'd have had to have found a buyer in August, when everyone was on holiday.

- **November**: generally too cold and miserable. People are thinking more about Christmas and want to hang on to their money.

- **December**: disastrous as a time to move. Very cold, damp and miserable, and what's more people are only thinking about Christmas. Who wants to celebrate Christmas amongst packing cases? Better wait until next year . . .

'Well, it seems a real bargain at the price.'

THE IDEAL HOUSE

Having moved, you will probably live in the new house for anything from five to 25 years. Clearly, therefore, you should ensure that the house you move to is the right house for you. Unfortunately, instead of making cool, rational decisions about houses, most people let their hearts rule their heads and take on a property which really meets very few of their needs. I would recommend sitting down quietly for half an hour to list your requirements *before* going to see any estate agents or reading any house details. The important thing is to avoid being seduced by the delightful country cottage in deepest Dorset, with roses rambling over the walls, views over a pretty water-meadow and half an acre of cottage garden, when what you really wanted was a two-bed flat off Kensington High Street. Once you have made your list, only then should you go ahead and let your heart rule your head (you're going to anyway – we all do).

The ideal house varies of course from person to person, and it is impossible in a book like this to give much in the way of concrete advice (except perhaps that you should avoid houses next to concrete factories). However, regardless of personal tastes, certain characteristics should apply to any 'ideal' house:

- it is warm, dry and free from pests, including double-glazing salesmen;
- it is easy and cheap to heat;
- it is in a pleasant area and with really nice neighbours;
- it is structurally sound;
- it is convenient for schools, shops, etc.;
- it is so close to your work that you can lean on your desk without having to get out of bed, yet so far from work that you are never pestered at home;
- it is so well insulated that even when it is −20°C outside, you can fry an egg on the floor inside without the heating on, and at anything above −50°C you need to leave most of the windows open in order not to die of heat prostration;
- yet, in summer, every room is as cool as a refrigerator;
- the house repaints itself every five years;
- household rubbish somehow disappears spontaneously;
- it costs only half what it should, but will double its value every two weeks, and is so saleable that you can guarantee finding a buyer within 10 minutes;
- your mother-in-law cannot find it;
- it has self-cutting grass;
- it is about as accessible to life insurance salesmen as the dark side of the moon, and about as hospitable to them;

'*Maybe* now *you'll* agree it was a false economy to buy a place under the
flight path!'

'It's a "Welcome to your new home" card from our neighbour . . .
apparently he's a glazier.'

Any house that meets these basic requirements, plus any special requirements specific to you as an individual, is probably worth seeing. If it meets
these criteria, then you can quite happily let your emotions take charge and
buy with the heart rather than the head.

- it has a vast hoard of gold bullion buried in the garden;
- all the dust gathers itself naturally in one corner ready for easy disposal;
- the neighbourhood is inhabited by scantily clad nymphets/Adonises (accord-
  ing to your wishes);
- it is only feet away from a charming pub that sells beer at a penny a pint, and
  gin and tonics at twopence;
- it commands a view that makes the Taj Mahal by moonlight look like a back
  street in Salford;
- it is totally exempt from rates;
- the electricity and gas boards like the house so much they don't send bills;
- it is so quiet at night that you can hear a pin drop in the next village five miles
  away. . . .
- yet, during the day, the neighbours are at all times willing to help with the
  most mundane and boring household chores (of which there aren't any);
- the rooms can be varied in shape to accommodate any item of furniture;
- the windows clean themselves on command.

ESTATE AGENTS' DETAILS

Having announced your intention of moving house to an estate agent, you will be immediately bombarded with details of thousands of houses, most of which will bear no resemblance at all to what you actually want. You will therefore need a rapid and efficient way of sifting out those properties worth a closer look from those that are not. It helps to understand the estate agent's language, which actually bears as much similarity to ordinary English as an ingrowing toenail does to a turbocharged 500 cc Honda. The estate agent's objective is, of course, to present the house in its very best light. The guide that follows should enable you to separate fiction from reality.

Room dimensions   Estate agents *never* underestimate the dimensions of a room unless they are totally inappropriate to its function (for example, a toilet which measures 45 x 34 feet). If a room is so small that even a 50 per cent exaggeration of its size still leaves it sounding pokey the dimensions will normally be omitted. Hence, if the dimensions of the sitting room are not given, whereas very precise details about the size and shape of the bathroom and garage are, beware this property; you can be sure that the sitting room won't take even one standard-size armchair. Also, if an agent *can* measure a room in its favour, be sure that he will, even if it involves climbing into the fireplace with one leg sticking out of the window and poking the tape measure into the central-heating vents. Some examples of how to interpret dimensions are given below:

- 14′6″ × 12′3″ . . .   13′9″ × 11′6″;
- approx. 14′6″ x 12′3″. . .   either 13′1″ x 11′2″ or the agent forgot to measure it, and so he is guessing, or he did measure it and it turned out to be even smaller than he feared;
- roughly 14′6″ x 12′3″. . .   the walls wouldn't stay still long enough to allow accurate measurement, or were too dangerous to approach closely, so a guess was made;
- 14′6″ x 12′3″ overall. . .   that it is 14′6″ x 12′3″ provided the tape measure goes over all the furniture;
- over 14′6″ long. . .   over 14′6″ with the measure over a couple of armchairs;
- around 14′6″ long. . .   with the tape around the legs of the chairs as well;

'I said it was a desirable detached . . . I didn't specify what.'

- 14′6″ max. × 12′3″. . .   the room is not square;
- 14′6″ × 12′3″ into alcove. . .   14′6″ × 6′1″ into everywhere else;
- 14′6″ × 12′3″ L-shaped. . .   two grotty narrow passages meeting at right angles;

- deceptively large. . .   it looks like 14′7″ × 12′4″, but is, amazingly, only 14′6″ × 12′3″;

- spacious. . .   it looks bigger (in the agent's mind) than mere physical dimensions can portray;

- very spacious. . .   the same as spacious but has one extra word and hence helps fill a line on the details;

- unusually large. . .   unusual and large;
- generously proportioned. . .   big in all the wrong directions, such as having a ceiling 45 feet high;

- cosy. . .   small;
- easily maintained. . .   pokey, and you can paint the ceiling whilst lying on your back on the floor;

- compact. . .   very pokey ('compact' is about the most damning thing any estate agent can say about a room).

Room uses   The house-buyer might naively expect a room to have a clearly defined and unique use. Estate agents however have a more creative approach to this issue, and this can result in a number of serious pitfalls for the potential buyer. Some examples are given below:

- Study/bedroom 4. . .   an estate agents' favourite, since it allows them to describe the same room twice in the details;

- Study/dining room. . .   a similar ploy to the previous one, but it suggests a slightly more cramped house overall;

- Garage/bathroom 2. . .   one of the subtle catches for the viewer to beware of;

- Kitchen/guest suite. . .   a combination guaranteed to ensure that no one comes to stay with you;

- Sitting room/toilet 3/ conservatory. . .   a sure danger sign;
- A useful room. . .   the agent is sure it has a use, but he can't for the life of him think what;

- Sun room/utility room/games room/family room. . .   these normally mean the same – a grotty, pokey, damp, nondescript room that you certainly couldn't *live* in. 'Sun room' means that it has a window; 'games room' means it doesn't.

Room descriptions   Similarly, the descriptions of the rooms need careful interpretation. Some of the more common examples include:

- Flexible accommodation   the floor sags;
- Airy. . .   there are holes in the walls;
- Comfortable. . .   the agent will be comfortable when he's got it off his hands;
- Adaptable accommodation. . .   the agent couldn't think what *he* would do with the rooms if he bought it;
- Finely proportioned. . .   odd-shaped;
- Room of character. . .   the room is old and dingy;
- Roomy. . .   the room has room-like qualities, which should come as no great surprise.

Condition of the structure   This is one real minefield on the house detail sheets. Some of the favourite descriptions used by agents include:

- in need of some improvement and updating. . .   it will require a virtually total rebuild;
- in need of restoration. . .   a total rebuild would be quicker and cheaper;
- in need of total restoration. . .   a total rebuild would be both quicker and cheaper, but no builder has yet been brave enough to go near it to give an estimate;
- with many interesting features. . .   the bits you would demolish first if you could get a builder;
- in good decorative order. . .   this is about the most basic comment an estate agent can make about any property, and can mean absolutely anything;
- well maintained. . .   there are still flakes of paint visible on the woodwork;
- immaculately maintained. . .   in some areas the flakes of paint meet in the middle;
- tastefully decorated. . .   the woodworm liked the taste of the paint and ate it all before starting on the wood;
- in need of decoration. . .   it is hard to establish whether or not the wood was *ever* painted;
- recently the subject of considerable expenditure. . .   you'd never guess the weird things they found to spend money on;
- artistically decorated   this is a real danger sign, suggesting that it might be best to view the house in total darkness;
- pleasant. . .   this is a euphemism for awful;
- charming. . .   this is a euphemism for pleasant;
- impressive. . .   this is a euphemism for charming;
- fine/imposing. . .   the agent hasn't actually seen the house in person;
- recently refurbished. . .   some considerable work has been done, but it still looks so awful that you'd never guess unless they told you.

The garden   In many cases the purchaser can be finally swayed by the garden. If the house is OK or so-so, but the garden has the basic appeal of the country cottage garden so ingrained in the British character, a sale can be virtually guaranteed. Agents are well aware of this, and describe gardens in an appropriately rosy way. For instance:

- Country style. . .   a jungle.
- Cottage style. . .   a small jungle.
- Planned for easy maintenance. . .   unbelievably small.
- Compact. . .   half the size of the smallest garden you could ever imagine.
- Manageable. . .   by Wimpey.
- Sunny. . .   the sun shines into the garden on at least

one day per year.

- Suit a gardening enthusiast. . .   only a real expert could think of anything that would actually grow there.

- Delightful south-facing. . .   means virtually nothing, as you can face south in any garden (even if you are then staring at a brick wall) and pretend to be delighted.

- Landscaped. . .   not flat.
- Professionally landscaped. . .   even the experts can make mistakes and produce a garden that isn't flat.
- Well stocked. . .   overgrown.
- Neat. . .   almost totally devoid of plants.
- Well screened. . .   the sun never shines into it.
- Private. . .   so overgrown that few people have ever penetrated it.
- Secluded. . .   no one can even find it.
- Mature. . .   wild.
- Spacious grounds. . .   a garden larger than 15 × 15 feet.
- Nearly half an acre. . .   the smaller half.

General features of the house   General comments which appear on estate agents' details often provide clues as to the real nature of a property. Some can add thousands to the asking price, others can mean that a trip to view the property would be a total waste of time. Among the phrases currently in vogue are these:

- Architect-designed. . .   presumably this helps the prospective purchaser establish that the property wasn't designed by a taxidermist, traffic warden or novelty hat manufacturer; a meaningless comment, usually indicating that the asking price is about £20,000 more than any sane person would offer.

- Built by a builder for his own occupation. . .   so why isn't he living in it now? Presumably, since he supposedly knows something about houses, he has concluded that it is no longer structurally safe. (Interestingly, if you added up the number of houses built by builders for their own occupation you'd probably find that half the entire population were so employed.)

- Built by a well-known local builder for his own occupation. . .   same as above, and the mistakes in the structure are well known locally.
- A rare opportunity to acquire. . .   people don't often have the nerve to put houses in this condition on the market.
- A listed building. . .   it is listed on the estate agent's secret blacklist.
- Period. . .   decrepit for its age.
- Suit a first-time buyer. . .   no one who has ever bought a house

'It's been a semi ever since no. 14 fell down the old mine workings.'

- A pied-à-terre. . .
  there's about enough room to put one foot on the floor.

- Investment opportunity. . .
  once it is sold the vendor will have lots of money to invest rather than a grotty old ruin.

- Executive development. . .
  think of an offer and add on £30,000: then you'll be only £20,000 short of the asking price.

- An improving area. . .
  located in a slum.

- Early viewing recommended. . .
  if you leave it any later it might have fallen down completely before you get there.

before would make the mistake of buying it.

Location Before making the effort to see the house, you will probably want to get a good idea of the location and area. This is one topic which really fires the imagination of the typical estate agent, and produces some truly poetic interpretations of the truth:

- The Thames. . .
  in spite of its highly specific geographical interpretation, the word Thames has special meaning to the estate agency business; specifically, it doubles the price on any property with such an address. Any town actually on the Thames will be so described – Marlow on Thames, Henley on Thames, Maidenhead on Thames, Goring on

'It was built by a builder for his own occupation . . . but he lost his nerve.'

Thames, etc. It does not matter that no one in these towns ever calls them by these names. But agents sometimes get a bit carried way, so you should be on the lookout for the more artistic descriptions such as High Wycombe near Thames, Dagenham on Thames, Slough just-down-the-road-from-the Thames, and even flights of pure fantasy like Salford on Thames. Strictly, you should beware of any house described as being 'on' the Thames when 'beside' is really what you want.

- Thames Valley. . .

if the agent is really quite honest, or the loction is really a bit far from the actual river to justify the magic 'on Thames' title, the fallback is to say 'Thames Valley'. But this requires careful interpretation: for instance, if the details simply say 'in the Thames Valley', it probably means Slough, whereas 'convenient for the Thames Valley' can mean anywhere from Swindon to Ongar. And in these days of high-speed travel 'near the Thames Valley' can imply almost anywhere from Dover to Inverness.

- Convenient for international businessmen. . .
  under the flight-path to Heathrow.
- Excellent communications. . .
  near a railway station, and usually so close that the house shakes to let you know when each train is approaching or departing.
- Ideal for commuter. . .
  in railway station forecourt.
- 10m to M4. . .
  10 minutes, 10 miles or 10 months, depending. . .
- Convenient for M4. . .
  the front door opens on to the hard shoulder.
- Walking distance of local amenities. . .
  there is a postbox within four miles.
- Select area. . .
  no one wants to live there.
- Quiet area. . .
  none of your friends will ever find the house.
- Much-sought-after area. . .
  much-sought-after but never found.
- Up-and-coming area. . .
  it is currently the absolute pits, and can *only* get better.
- Favoured area. . .
  favoured by someone, but God knows who.
- Improving area. . .
  the asking price is about twice what a sane person would pay for a house in such a slum.
- Rural. . .
  there are trees and grass everywhere.
- Semi-rural. . .
  the trees and grass are outside the house only.
- Established area. . .
  the drawbacks of the area are there to stay.
- Favoured western side of town. . .
  they did not say which town.

Danger signs Some additional phrases to beware of:

- Level walk to shops. . .
  my God, if 'level walk' is a selling point think how hilly it must *really* be – or how few other advantages the house is likely to have.
- Purpose-built. . .
  for what purpose, other than living in? Was it designed as an abattoir?
- Well above river level. . .
  you can be pretty sure the level of the river is pretty variable; or it could mean that there is a well in the garden from which it is difficult to get water.

'. . . and it's within a stone's throw of local schools.'

- Away from the flight-path. . .   not under the flight-path on about one day a year.

- Ideal second home. . .   no one would tolerate living in it *all* the time.

- Ideal holiday home. . .   two weeks is about the longest any sane person could stay there.

- Ideal retirement home. . .   once you have bought it you will never be able to sell it again.

- Within stone's throw of local schools. . .   half the windows are broken every month.

- Sheltered location. . .   overshadowed by tower blocks.
- Private road. . .   even the council could not find it in order to adopt the road.

- Individual. . .   the architect was shot after it was built to ensure he could never make the same sort of mistake again.

- Sole agent. . .   no other estate agent had the faintest hope of selling it.

- Unexpectedly re-available. . .   the last buyer found out just in time.
- Realistically priced. . .   priced at only twice what it is really worth, but has some ghastly snag.

Rateable value   The rateable value is worthy of note in so far as it is probably the single reliable piece of information you will ever extract from the typical estate agent. Unfortunately its practical value is limited, for unless you know the rate in the pound imposed by the local authority it does not tell you what rates you will actually need to pay.

'. . . and as you see, it's in perfect structural condition . . .'

'*As I said, it looks just like the photo.*'

HOUSE PHOTOGRAPHS

In estate agents' windows, and on the details they send to you, you'll find enticing photographs of properties they want you to buy. Prospective purchasers, especially first-time buyers, should however take care to avoid the common mistake of believing that what they see in the photo bears any resemblance at all to the house in question. The real house and the photograph probably have about as much in common as an armadillo and an after-dinner mint. Photographers employed by estate agents are masters of deception. Indeed, it often happens that viewers drive up and down the same road half a dozen times looking for the impressive-looking property depicted on the details only to discover in the end that this desirable property is actually the pokey little hovel in the drive of which they've just completed six three-point turns, and demolition of which would considerably enhance the area. You'll find it easier to locate most properties if you forget the photograph and just work from the address.

The magic of many of these photographs lies in the estate agent's best friend, the wide-angle lens. About 60 per cent of all wide-angle lenses, I would estimate, are sold to estate agents' photographers. The secret of the wide-angle lens is that it can make a narrow, broken, 15-foot-long drive look like a majestic approach to a country house – 250 yards long, 40 feet wide and (with the help of a little re-touching) in immaculate condition. Similarly, it can make the neighbours' houses look as if they are 200 feet away when in fact they are so close that you have to take turns opening the windows. It is sometimes easy to spot the wide-angle photograph, through give-aways such as the Ford Escort which stretches away to the side of the picture and looks at least 45 feet long, or of which you can see all four sides at the same time.

In addition to the wide-angle trick, the prospective purchaser should be on the lookout for a number of other danger signs.

- the house is shown in a snowy setting but the details are sent out in August (equally, if viewing in winter look out for pictures which show daffodils and tulips): this is one of the best indicators of what estate agents call a non-rapidly advancing purchase situation scenario (or a bloody pig of a property to sell);

- smudgy backgrounds (it's amazing what a stiff brush can do in the dark room): that faint tree might actually be a cooling tower;

- the photograph shows only the back or side of the house;

- only interior views are shown, in colour: if this is the case, the outside *must* be pretty awful, or maybe the photographer couldn't get far enough away to take a picture because of neighbours' cars parked outside;

- photographs which stop about 6 inches above ground level: there may be no clearly defined ground as such, just an unplanned lake;

- the photograph has that give-away flat look of the telephoto shot taken from half a mile away: it could be that the smell is so bad that that is the nearest the photographer could bear to be;

- the picture is cut square, has its corners cut off or is trimmed to lozenge shape – a sure sign of trouble; and if the walls appear parallel to the edges of the frame, but the picture is way off true, then subsidence could be a problem;

- the house is not placed in the middle of the picture, but cowers instead at one edge, or even in one small corner: this could mean some unpleasant surprises are in store;

- bushes dominate the foreground to the virtual exclusion of the property itself;

- the photo does not show all of the house: if it only shows one window, or the front door, or even worse just one of the drain covers, then take special care when viewing to look for the hidden snags;

- a black and white photograph instead of a colour one: this could conceal a multitude of sins, such as a fetching yellow and purple colour scheme for the exterior walls and paintwork.

REAL DANGER SIGNS

'For pity's sake don't take down the "For Sale" sign . . . it's holding up the house.'

In most cases, when things go badly wrong in a house move, the people concerned only have themselves to blame. Instead of entering the deal with their eyes wide open, aware of all the potential pitfalls, they shut their eyes to any snags and let their heads be totally ruled by their hearts. Most of the real problems are there for all to see, if only the purchasers were prepared to accept that the house of their dreams might be something less than perfect.

Try to view the house in bright daylight, when it is raining, when the vendor is there in person, and try to view on more than one day of the week. I remember one quiet Sunday afternoon seeing a house that looked like a bargain – an old rectory, in a perfect tranquil setting. The following day I was on my way to put an offer on it when, as if driven by some powerful subconscious force, I called round for another quick look – only to discover that the innocent little old brick building next door contained a 40-ton steam-hammer which, from 8.00 am every Monday until 5.00 pm every Friday, made the rectory practically leave the ground every 8 seconds. Since that time I have always made a point of viewing houses on a weekday.

Listed below are some of the real danger signs potential house purchasers should be on the lookout for when viewing a house:

- large areas of clearly still-wet mortar or plaster;
- damp patches on the ceilings;
- the vendor frisks you on the way into the house;
- the Rentokil guarantee is prominently displayed in a silver frame over the fireplace;
- you are only allowed to view the house after dark and in dry weather;
- the furniture is all nailed to the floor;
- the estate agent operates from a phonebox;
- the vendor presses you for a *very* quick sale . . . for instance, within the next ten minutes, and starts begging you on all fours to make any offer over £1;
- policemen are digging up the garden;
- the vendor clearly lives in a tent in the garden;
- the vendor answers the door wearing waders, a hard hat, ear plugs or a false beard;
- the vendor expresses excessive surprise that you turned up at all;
- there are aeroplane-tyre marks or scorch marks on the roof;
- the vendor keeps an inflatable dingy or parchute next to the front door;
- you are asked to walk only near the walls;
- the vendor clearly prefers you to go upstairs one at a time, and doesn't volunteer to come with you;
- the vendor offers to show you a video of the upstairs rather than letting you go up there yourself;
- the vendor stands at the far end of the garden whenever you go up the stairs;
- the vendor asks you about personal accident insurance cover before letting you in;
- the garden is being surveyed by the Ministry of Transport;
- whenever you turn up to view there is a gang of tired-looking scaffolders and a large heap of scaffolding outside in the road, and the foreman is on his knees praying;
- the walls are covered from floor to ceiling with paintings screwed in place;
- every room contains a wooden stake and has a bunch of garlic hanging at the doors and windows.

CHOOSING A SOLICITOR

'Good news! I've found a surveyor brave enough to take a look at The Pines!'

When it comes to choosing a solicitor to carry out conveyancing on a house move, most people turn to the *Yellow Pages*, consult friends and relatives, or of course go to a solicitor they have used in the past. Some wise people shop around extensively to get the best bargain, and certainly this can result in impressive savings (however, look out for false bargains: be suspicious of any solicitor who offers to deal with a purchase and sale for £2.75 plus a pint and a fag). But how should we select a lawyer for this task? And do we really need to be choosy at all?

In fact, conveyancing is not the most challenging of legal activities. Rarely does purchasing a house call for extensive and probing cross-examination of a hostile witness under oath (except where the vendor is exceptionally reticent about his intentions concerning bathroom fittings), challenging the integrity of jurors, applications for extradition orders on Peruvian exiles, or appeals to the House of Lords or European Court of Justice (although the issue of fitted carpets can often generate emotions which might suggest this course of action). Rather, the major skills needed

'Well, The Larches is all yours now . . . well, all that's left of it, that is . . .'

are those of sticking postage stamps the right way up, folding letters (albeit in the rather strange elongated shape so beloved of the legal profession), answering telephones without falling off the chair and concussing oneself, and writing out extortionate bills. The majority of practising solicitors can accomplish these tasks after about three years' training; and after a further four years or so in actual practice they can normally accomplish all four tasks on the same day (although judging from some of the excuses I was given for delays the last time we moved, this is not that easy to believe).

Professional expertise is therefore rarely a constraint and plays little part in your task of selecting the right lawyer. However, the basic requirements for legal practice should guarantee a certain minimum level of competence; they are as follows:

- a degree in law (although 48-inch biceps go some way towards compensating for any lack of formal qualifications);

- being admitted by the Law Society (although what they are supposed to admit about the solicitor is never revealed, and the suspicion may tend to linger);

- a brass plate (affording the brass plate is often the most difficult bit of setting up in practice);

- two sheets of paper and a paper clip to hold them together;

- one exceptionally long and narrow manilla envelope to put the paper inside;

- the ability to remain sober enough for long enough to write on the paper and post it to someone.

With these basic essentials the solicitor is in business for conveyancing. But given that any real solicitor should possess these, we need to look at other factors when making our choice. The following characteristics are without doubt desirable;

- he or she should not smell excessively rank (of course you don't have to meet your solicitor face to face, in which case olefactory considerations take less importance; but if you don't meet, take special care to avoid solicitors who insist on all correspondence being left under unmarked stones beside quiet country roads or take all phone calls from call boxes. Also, check letters for Parkhurst postmarks);

- he or she should look business-like and have an office full of leather-bound volumes;

- he or she should not behave suspiciously: the odd eccentricity is OK, but beware solicitors who hide behind their desk pleading, 'It wasn't me!';

- he or she should not appear excessively kinky: the mild eccentricity such as leather handkerchiefs, shiny black vinyl memo pads and rubber trousers, should have little real impact on professional competence, but be on the lookout for more serious deviations from normality such as an admiration for tax inspectors, a belief in the reliability of the Range Rover, or credence in the sayings of Members of Parliament;

- he or she should be generally familiar with house sale and purchase. Again this is not essential, but it is certainly useful if the solicitor knows what the word 'conveyancing' means (or has access to a good dictionary); if the words 'house' and 'sale' cause problems you might have made a wrong choice.

UNDERSTANDING SOLICITORS

'Yes, I can do conveyancing for you . . . whatever that is.'

Conveyancing is actually a very simple process requiring about the same degree of intellectual input from the solicitor as deciding what he should have on his toast at breakfast-time. However, in order to preserve their professional image (and justify their charges), it is necessary for solicitors to surround the whole subject with technical jargon. This can take some understanding from the uninitiated. Listed below are some of the phrases you are likely to encounter.

- Conveyancing: a complicated-sounding word for filling in a couple of forms which any intelligent 11-year-old could cope with (but couldn't charge £600 for); conveyancing actually means conveying money from your bank account to the solicitor's.

- Legal document: actually just a piece of paper, but one for which you paid about £100 per square inch.

- In conference with a client: down at the pub.

- Detained in chambers: in the loo at the pub.

- Subject to contract: means things can still go badly wrong, which might mean much higher legal fees (especially if that holiday in the Bahamas turns out to be more expensive than first thought).

- Local searches: these are what the solicitor does if he has lost all the documents.

- Without prejudice: means things can still go badly wrong, but the solicitor doesn't want to get blamed for it.

- Draft contract: this is an excuse for drawing up more than one contract so that the solicitor can charge twice as much (why a trial run at a contract is required, God knows).

- Daft contract: often an uncannily true malapropism in the form of a typing error.

- Acting for X: means X pays the bill.

- Professional services: the reason why X will pay so much.

- Land Registry Search: something that sounds important, indispensible and horribly expensive, but probably means nothing at all, but for which X will pay £45: a good excuse for jacking up the bill.

- Seized in fee simple: a ghastly-sounding state of affairs, which again is likely to cost a lot of money to put right.

'Under normal circumstances failure to provide vacant possession would merely result in a financial penalty . . .'

- Final searches: a reason for adding a final 10 per cent to the bill.

- Disbursements: another word for money, but one which sounds less greedy.

- Fees: a word for money which is more frank than disbursements but less frank than 'bill'.

- Charges: the closest reference you'll get to the fact that they want all your cash.

- Technicalities: this is an umbrella term to cover a multitude of problems (for example, all the documents' being ruined when the solicitor's umbrella dripped on to them).

- Complications: bad technicalities which, if the truth got out, might result in the solicitor being struck off.

- Serious complications: he already has been struck off but thought (mistakenly) that he might get away with it.

- Our most experienced conveyancer: the tea-boy.

- Senior partner: a crusty, senile ruin who charges twice what any of the other solicitors does because he's kept alive on gin-and-tonic.

- Chambers: offices.

- Office: dump.

- Will receive our immediate attention: will be promptly forgotten about.

- Has just been put in the post: we forgot about it but will put it in the post this afternoon.

- On my desk right now: I had forgotten about it but feel quite guilty.

- The post is so slow this week: I had forgotten, but you might buy the 'stupid old GPO' trick.

'Be frank with me . . . . conveyancing doesn't turn you on like it used to, does it?'

THE CAMPAIGN FOR REAL CONVEYANCING

Just as the serious drinker has come to seek a more traditional type of beer, the so-called 'real' ale (or ghastly flat ale as many believe), many solicitors have started to hark after the good old days when men were men, Japanese cars were sold in Japan, aubergines hadn't been heard of, you could still hear Spanish spoken on the Costa del Sol, and fags were 1*s* 6*d* for 20. This is how the as yet little-known Campaign for Real Conveyancing started. The main aims of the Campaign are to restore a legal profession in which:

- all fees are quoted in guineas, and paid in gold coins carried in velvet purses;

- all written work is executed using a quill pen, and ink is blotted with sand;

- all offices are oak-panelled;

- all contracts are prepared on vellum and rolled up as a scroll.

- no clerk earns more than 14*s* 6*d* per week (it is believed that this is the main motivation behind the campaign);

- only hand-made paper or parchment is used;

- contracts are prepared only when a swirling mist shrouds the cobbled streets outside;

- contracts are delivered either on horseback or by hansom cab;

- all written work is carried out by candle- or gas-light;

- all clerks are called by names such as Digby, Oliver or Tobias;

- all staff dress in tailcoats and wear high collars;

- pictures of the property included with house details are original miniatures painted in oils;

- house details begin with an illuminated capital;

- viewers are conveyed to the properties by sedan chair;

- fees remain at current levels, of course.

The Campaign believes that a house can only be declared 'sold' if these guidelines have been followed.

'You could either repair the leaks for £5000 or turn it into an indoor
swimming-pool for £6000.'

SURVEYORS' REPORTS

If you want to be put off buying a house for life, simply read a surveyor's report. Many people take what they think is the wise precaution of getting a structural surveyor to examine a house before they reach the point of no return in buying the property. However, few realize what a traumatic experience they are in for once the long-awaited report arrives through the post (I can't imagine how structural surveyors themselves ever find a suitable house to live in; do they lie awake at nights worrying about rising damp, defective rainwater goods or decaying sarking felt? Maybe they don't; maybe they all live in tents instead). To maximize your chances of surviving the experience, heed the following recommendations:

Before opening the report:

- sit down in a comfortable chair and loosen all tight clothing;

- open a bottle of good Scotch and drink the first half;

- try not to be alone;

- if in any doubt about your physical condition, go to your doctor for a medical check-up first;

- take ten deep breaths;

- if you have any lingering worries, tear up the report straight away.

You should then be ready to digest the report. This requires care, as you have to bear in mind that it is the surveyor's job to find faults. No surveyor is going to report 'a nice little semi, just right for you, the wife and kids to settle down in', because this would be an admission of defeat. Surveyors take fault-finding as a challenge. No surveyor has ever been known to find a house perfect: a house that *looks* perfect is just better at hiding its defects than most. There follow some examples of the type of content and language to be found in surveyors' reports (each taken from the report I received on the house I currently occupy . . . that is, until it falls down, which is almost certain judging from the surveyor's comments), together with an idea of the true meaning and interpretation.

(In the general comments on the structure): *'significant hairline cracks, diagonal in nature, in the rear offside corner of the property could indicate incipient structural subsidence necessitating at some time in the future extensive underpinning; but without examining the structure over a protracted period of* *time it is impossible to ascertain the true nature of the problem. However on balance the risk is acceptable'*: this is *really* comforting! It is nice to know that, on balance, the risk of the whole structure collapsing under your feet into a pile of dust and flinging you homeless out on to the street is *acceptable*. Acceptable to whom, I ask? (In reality such comments simply mean that the house is in perfectly average condition.)

(In the comments about the roof): *'the roof structure is framed in softwood with common rafters spanning from ridge hip boards to softwood wall plates, lateral support being provided by ceiling joists and softwood ties to adjacent gable, and midspan support by purlins which unfortunately do not transfer loads effectively to the structure beneath. However the absence of any sag in the roof structure suggests that support is adequate'*: does this mean the roof is going to remain on top of the house or not? Just how soft is the soft wood, and are the rafters just too common to be acceptable in the neighbourhood? (In reality these comments really just say that the house *has* a roof.)

'The house is constructed of brick under a tiled roof.' Do you mean I paid £550 to be told the house is built of brick and the roof is made of tiles? My 7-year-old son could have told me that for free! Was the surveyor worried that I thought the bricks were cunningly disguised shortbread biscuits, and the tiles were really pieces of toast?

At the end, the inevitable disclaimer: *'those parts of the property which are concealed, inaccessible or covered have not been inspected and it cannot be recorded that such parts are free from timber decay or other defects'.* Great – so the deathwatch beetle simply hid under the carpet, enabling the surveyor to avoid any blame! What parts of the house *were* hidden or inaccessible, for Christ's sake? I wouldn't have worried if he hadn't disclaimed responsibility. Surely he must suspect *something* to go to the bother of typing it?

After two hours of digesting comments such as these, the only sane thing to do is consume the other half of the whisky, tear up the report, pay the man's bill, shout, 'Sod it!!!', and just move!

'Any normal person would have been suspicious of a solicitor offering conveyancing for £2.50 and a bottle of gin.'

'*It's subsidence.*'

'Do you want to pay extra for the five-star service, or don't you mind if a few things get broken?'

CHOOSING A REMOVAL FIRM

When you come to move house, it is important to choose a removal firm which will look after your belongings. This need not necessarily mean going to one of the major international companies. The small local man can be just as good, if not better, if you choose carefully. Ideally, go for a firm which has successfully moved a friend or relative; failing that, ask for references and don't be afraid to take them up. The basic essentials for removal firms go slightly beyond the matter of sheer physical strength; they also need a certain degree of intelligence in order to know where various items should be put, and how to get those difficult pieces up narrow stairs and through awkward doorways.

As a general guide, avoid removal companies:

- whose men always wear balaclava helmets or ladies' stockings over their heads;
- which offer references from the Pope;
- whose vans carry L-plates;
- whose van has the name painted out;
- which insist on moving you at 2 am in the morning;
- whose vans have chain-saws in the cab;
- whose vans have bits of pianos lying around all over the place;
- which only let you examine their removal vans blindfolded;
- which turn up with skips or a dump truck instead of a pantechnicon;

- which quote you a price without even asking to see the house or effects;

- which refer to your belongings as 'loot';

- whose name, painted on the side of the van, is still wet;

- whose van has its number plate covered up;

- which quote you a price before you've even told them you want to move house;

- which offer to pay for the privilege of moving you;

- whose vans show clear signs of having carried cattle;

- whose vans constantly cruise round the block whilst the manager operates from an orange crate on the pavement;

- whose van bears the legend 'Used Furniture Salesman';

- whose drivers wear crash helmets or fireproof overalls;

- which put lot numbers or price tags on your furniture;

- which emphasize the benefits of putting the piano in the bathroom.

Some firms will not only move your effects, but will also offer, for a charge, to pack everything as it stands and move it all to the new house and unpack it, so all you have to do is vacate the house in the morning and remember to return home to a different address in the evening. In addition to these extra services, some firms will attempt to attract your business by means of impressive-sounding qualifications such as:

'Hello, I'm your new neighbour. Can you lend me 50 quid?'

- FRSFR (Fellow of the Royal Society of Furniture Removers)
- FRSPS (Fellow of the Royal Society of Piano Shifters)
- PhD in china- and crockery-packing
- DSO (Distinguished Shifting Order)
- By Appointment to His Highness King Peter of Bothuania, Removers of Personal Effects and Things
- VC (Very Careful).

Of course, no matter how good the removal firm, there is no guaranteeing that nothing will go wrong on the day of removal. In some cases the removal van doesn't turn up at all, or the van turns up, is loaded up with your effects, and you never see them again; then you face the prospect of living in a completely empty house. At the other extreme you may forget on the crucial day where your new house is, and face the prospect of living in the removal van for the rest of your life; whilst inconvenient, this does at least have the advantage that you'll save on rates, and you can enjoy a pleasant change of scenery each day.

Between these extremes are a whole spectrum of problems such as extensive damage to furniture, or demolition of the house when the brakes on the van fail; in the latter case you face an interesting dilemma – whether to live in the wreck of the van or the rubble of the house. And, of course, even if the move itself is a success, you still won't know whether your furniture is going to fit into the new house, or even squeeze through the front door; if it doesn't, you face the exciting challenge of sleeping in the garage – or playing the piano in the loo.

Finally, if all the risks of employing a removal firm sound just a bit too much, you can always choose to move yourself. But be warned: if you are crazy enough to consider this, you are too crazy to carry on reading this book (and that's saying something!).

'A thousand years old, eh . . .? Lucky it wasn't a new one, missus.'

APPLYING FOR A LOAN

The overwhelming majority of people need a loan in order to buy a house, and most will go to a bank or a building society. How you actually go about applying for the loan can strongly influence your chances of getting it, and can even affect the amount you get.

Most banks and building societies will insist upon a personal interview before granting you a loan, especially if the loan is a large one. Your attitude and approach towards this interview will have a strong influence on the outcome, and any conditions attached to the money. For example, if you are pleasant, straightforward and honest there is no reason why you should not end up borrowing 3 times the higher salary plus once the lower salary up to a maximum of £100,000, repayable over 25 years; on the other hand if you are unpleasant, devious and dishonest you may end up with a loan of 3 times the higher salary plus once the lower salary up to a maximum of £100,000 so long as you never step on the join between paving stones, never wear red underwear, don't go to the toilet when the date is an odd number, and repay the loan over a period of 25 minutes.

Basically, you should be neither too confident nor too timid; marching in, sitting on the desk with your feet on the manager's lap, patting him on the cheek and saying 'Right, tosh, how's about some dough then?' is almost as bad as shuffling in with a paper bag over your head, whimpering like a puppy, and pleading, 'Please, Mummy, give your little tootsie-kins a little loanie!' Neither approach will have you moving into that exclusive 5-bed detached in Surrey.

Some general guidelines about how to conduct the interview are outlined below.

- Go in person. Sending someone else, such as your probation officer, your mother-in-law, the vicar, your neighbour or your dog, will certainly count against you.

- Be honest on your application form. Although doctors, solicitors, civil servants, etc. may have higher standing when it comes to raising finance than pop singers, drag queens and stuntmen, there is no point in lying about your occupation. If you say you are a High Court judge but have a Mohican haircut, live in a rented bed-sit and confess to being on probation, then there is a chance your pretence might be rumbled.

- If you must lie, then lie consistently. For example, if you claim to be a cardinal, don't enter your wife's earnings on the form or claim that you make £250 per week with overtime.

- Go to the interview sober, and try to remain that way. Avoid at all costs swigging rough gin straight from a dirty bottle when the manager is asking about your state of health. If you *must* drink gin, wipe the mouth of the bottle first and offer the manager the first swig; if he declines, don't push it, and avoid forcibly pouring it into his mouth.

- Dress neatly and smartly. Don't dress over-smart; for example, morning coat and top hat is a bit excessive, as is full-dress uniform for members of the armed forces. Even more important, don't under-dress; don't go naked unless you are 100 per cent sure of getting a favourable response, and even in hot weather avoid bathing costumes.

- Don't grovel, whimper, slobber, moan, wet yourself, cry or pray. And leave teddy bears and security blankets at home.

- Don't attempt to bribe the manager; it's not his money he's lending you (unless you are exceptionally persuasive, that is).

- Appear understanding, clean, decent and law-abiding.

- Don't take a bag of fish and chips in with you.

- Don't take dogs, small kids, rabbits, hamsters, etc. with you.

- Don't remove your socks and start trimming your toenails.

- Don't bite, scratch, hiss or vomit if things don't go totally your way.

- Don't take a holdall to carry the cash away in. Things don't happen that way, with banks and building societies.

'Don't sorry . . . the house will be fine when the chaps come to clear the drain.'

WHOM TO GO TO FOR A LOAN

'Good afternoon . . . I'm your new neighbour.'

There are many different sources of finance for buying a house. Basically anyone with the right amount of money to spare and who won't change his mind and insist on having the money back on a whim (for example, having it back in used fivers on a silver plate on 25 seconds' warning) is a potential source of mortgage finance; it certainly helps if he is also pleasant, friendly and easy to see. Beware of anyone who offers you a loan in the form of 10p coins, or who insists on your being blindfolded before signing the mortgage agreement, or who communicates entirely by means of handwritten notes in plain brown envelopes left in left-luggage lockers at Euston Station. Some of the alternative sources of finance include:

'Even if the Home Office lets you buy the jail, I don't think the local authority
would let you demolish the walls.'

- building societies: the commonest choice for the small- to medium-sized loan. Will probably expect you to be a saver;

- banks: good for the medium-sized or larger loan, and can be quicker since they don't work to monthly allocations;

- Bank of England: only interested in large loans, and may be subject to government approval. A drawback for savers is that there is only one branch;

- International Monetary Fund: best for the really large loan (exceeding £300 million), but getting an interview can be difficult, and it tends to show little interest in three-bed semis in Watford;

- clairvoyants: can't usually lend a large sum, but can tell you in advance whether your application will be successful or not;

- local authority: a good choice for the smaller loan, or for loans on properties which are 'difficult' (for example, built on the hard shoulder of the M25);

- mother-in-law: good in the sense that she is unlikely to turn you down flat, but bad in the sense that the conditions attached to the loan are likely to be prohibitively punitive (such as coming to lunch every Sunday, spending every Christmas and Easter at her house, and taking her daughter out for a meal twice a week, conditions which are rare with building society managers);

- Oxfam: bad for big loans, but good for small loans (e.g. 25p) if you are really desperate for a home and it is in the right location (Ethiopia, Somalia, Chad, Basingstoke, etc.);

- local fish-and-chip shop: not really a good prospect as a source of finance (unless you are exceptionally persuasive) but if you are going to get turned down anyway, why not get turned down in a place where you can at least get a good, hot, cheap meal?

- the Pope: will probably expect you to be a practising Catholic, and so probably a better bet for the house suited to the larger family; generally not the best choice, but is likely to be quite charming when turning you down and may throw in a blessing as consolation;

- Salvation Army: better for small loans (about 20p–50p) and may even throw in the price of a cup of tea; unlike banks and building societies they do not generally expect the money to be repaid;

- Joan Collins: almost certainly won't lend you money, but one of the best people to approach for virtually anything even if a rejection results;

- your next-door neighbours: not a good choice unless you are very confident of success, as a rejection could lead to friction in the future; if your current neighbours fall over themselves in the race to lend you £40,000 to move, then you might conclude that you are not the most popular residents in the street;

- the Mafia: good for the really difficult loan (for example, where the owner doesn't want to sell, or where he has a ridiculously inflated idea of the property's value, in excess of, say, £25), but may be difficult to contact.

'*In that price bracket you get your own details out of the drawer.*'

HOW MUCH WILL YOU BE ABLE TO BORROW?

As a general rule, if you approach a building society or bank for a mortgage the amount you will be able to borrow will depend upon your ability to repay the loan. Normally the amount will be about three times the major income in the household plus the other income once. However, certain special circumstances may alter the total size of advance. The following formula may be taken as a guide:

Amount of loan =

        3 × major income of household
+   1 × minor income of household
+   £5000 if you are 6 feet 6 inches, weigh 18 stone and look *real* mean,
+   £5000 if you know where the manager went on holiday last spring when he was supposed to be at a conference. . .
+   £4000 if you know with whom he went. . .
+   £8000 if you know what was inside the strange brown parcel that was delivered by special messenger to the hotel room. . .
+   £6000 if you know why the special messenger stayed to join in the fun. . .
+   £2000 if you know what position he spent most of the evening in,
−   £6000 if the house you wish to buy is significantly better than the manager's own
+   £3000 if the house is the one the manager himself is trying desperately to sell

−   £1000 for any strange stains on your trousers
−   £6000 if you become visibly sexually excited at the mention of endowments
−   £3000 if you ask to see the manager's own endowments without his having first offered
−   £1000 for each of green socks, suede shoes, sandals, etc.
−   £8000 if you turn up wearing clothes for the wrong sex

−   £2000 if you have a dewdrop hanging from the end of your nose. . .
−   £1000 more if you wipe the dewdrop on the manager's sleeve.

'Forget the coffee, Miss Wilkins . . . his ceiling is only £40,000.'

CHOOSING AN ESTATE AGENT

There is usually no shortage of estate agents to choose from. Most big towns have estate-agent ghettos, in which the eye is bombarded by colour photographs of desirable houses with ludicrous asking prices. Choosing an agent is a bit like Russian roulette, except that in the latter case you have a five-out-of-six chance of winning. Since no qualifications are required to set up as an agent, it can be difficult to ensure that the one you go to is reputable. Often you can tell a lot from the name and style: for example, a solid name like D'Arcy, Travis Wymondham & Partners, operating from a mahogany-panelled office next to Lloyds Bank and staffed by distinguished middle-aged gentlemen in pinstripes may be a safer bet than an agent entitled Honest John's House Emporium operating from the back of a used-car lot and staffed by a teenaged skinhead called Wayne. The basic skills for an estate agent are:

- the ability to accept large amounts of money as commission without feelings of guilt, even if the sale required no more than a 25-second phone call;

- the ability to speak, or at least mumble convincingly, whilst smiling sweetly at the prospective buyer or seller;

- the strength to hammer a 'For Sale' sign into the ground, or sufficient hold over someone who is strong enough to make him do it for you;

- the ability to pick up a telephone with one hand whilst jotting down with the other the laughably low maximum price mentioned by your prospective purchaser without tittering;

- the ability to hand out sheets of paper at such a speed that the prospective purchaser loses control of his faculties, drops them all on the floor and feels small;

- the ability to remain continent at key moments;

- enough dexterity to fold A4 sheets in half, put them in envelopes and stick stamps on;

- a natural flair for sending people only details of properties that fall outside their price range;

- an ability to measure a room to within 50 per cent of its real dimensions.

This is clearly not a tall order, although a moist tongue and freehold possession of (or a time-sharing intercst in) a tape measure would clearly be an advantage (interestingly, there are few jobs outside the pornography

'The last time we had a house in your price range was back in 1921.'

trade where you can pick up a commission of £2000 on the strength of a moist tongue). If you *can't* find an agent with these essential skills, you might have a real problem selling your house.

Given the lack of formal qualifications and low ability levels necessary, you may well end up choosing on the basis of peripheral, more personal, features. Some of the more desirable features for a satisfactory agent include:

- clean underwear;
- a vivid imagination – for seeing the real potential in your broken-down hovel;
- a minimal criminal record, or at least a high degree of discretion;
- the ability to remain sober most of the time;
- no smell;
- a warm office with a spare seat;
- a warm office with a spare seat and lots of randy, nubile young women (or men, depending upon the sex and preferences of the prospective purchaser);
- an attractive window display in a convenient location;
- a persuasive but not pushy nature;
- not being related to your wife in a maternal sense.

'Of course you can *buy it for £35,000 . . . but wouldn't you rather live in a £135,000 house?'*

By contrast, some agents exhibit less favourable characteristics, such as:

- drawing the blinds before showing you any house details;
- wearing monk's or nun's habits and communicating entirely by means of Gregorian chant (unless this sort of thing turns you on);
- keeping house details in a locked safe;
- insisting on commission being paid in used £1 notes;
- providing only handwritten details;
- providing no written details at all, but conducting all business by whispered verbal means;
- preferring to meet you on the hard shoulder of the M4 after dark;
- insisting on blindfolding you before taking you to see a property;
- wearing balaclava helmets at all times;
- giving you sodium pentathol before taking down the details of your house;
- offering to do a quick tarmac job on your drive or extract any spare teeth on the cheap;
- calling you 'Petal', 'Flower', 'Toe-rag', 'Fart-bag', or any similar term of endearment;
- collapsing on the floor in hysterical laughter when you tell them your price ceiling.

'Of course, you're free to withdraw your offer on no. 12 . . .'

Some agents will attempt to impress you with a string of letters after their names. Essentially there are two real qualifications which are of value: some form of membership of the Royal Institute of Chartered Surveyors, and affiliation of the Society of Valuers and Auctioneers. In practice neither qualification is of much real value in selling houses, but they sound good and at least demonstrate that the agent can read and write. Some of the letters you may find include:

ARICS	Associate of the Royal Society of Chartered Surveyors.
FRICS	Fellow of the Royal Society of Chartered Surveyors.
IRICS	Inebriate of the Royal Society of Chartered Surveyors.
FFRICS	Formerly a Fellow of the Royal Society of Chartered Surveyors.
LRICS	Layabout of the Royal Society of Chartered Surveyors.
HRICS	Hanger-on of the Royal Society of Chartered Surveyors.
LNDTSWWFRICS	Lives Next Door to Someone Who Was a Fellow of Royal Society of Chartered Surveyors.

'I sent your offer on The Laurels straight to the BBC's Comedy Department.'

FSVA	Fellow of Society of Valuers and Auctioneers.
FSVT	Fellow of Society of Valuers and Taxidermists.
FSVTCP	Fellow of Society of Valuers, Taxidermists, Chiropodists and Plumbers.
BA Cantab	Born Around Cambridge.
MA Oxon	Mother Arrested in Oxford.
FRS	Farmed in Rural Suffolk.
PhD	Phoney Diploma.
LLB	Likes Large Bills.
DFC	Distinguished Fleecing Certificate.
CBE	Charges Bogus Expenses.

However, the best way of selecting an agent is to find someone who has had a pleasant experience with a particular one, and go to him or her; of course, it depends to some degree on what the pleasant experience was, whether the house was sold as a result, whether it was legal and within the spirit of the Geneva Convention, and whether it formed the start of a lasting and meaningful relationship.

'. . . and just wait till you see the sunken bath I've just installed . . .'

SALE DETAILS
FOR YOUR OWN HOUSE

One of the most sobering aspects of moving house is reading the details about your existing dwelling prepared by the estate agent. Most people, upon reading the agent's description (or fairy story), begin to wonder why they ever even *thought* about moving. Every estate agent can make your existing house sound like the most desirable residence ever to be offered to an ungrateful public (indeed it is not unknown for people to rush round to the estate agents and put substantial offers on their own houses just on the strength of the printed details). In view of this it is best never to read the details about your own house. Some of the examples you might encounter are summarized below:

- the garden becomes 'grounds', even if it only measures 15 × 15 feet. And if the lawn is not flat you will find it has become 'landscaped grounds' (presumably because it resembles a lunar landscape);

- and if the garden is even smaller it becomes 'easily maintained';

- the garden is, by definition, 'south-facing': presumably this means that if you stand in the garden (regardless of its actual orientation) you can, with the help of a compass, at least *face* south at some point; the fact that you may then be staring straight at a brick wall is, of course, quite beside the point;

- the old broken-down trellis-work you never got round to removing, and which caused a big row between you and your wife, has become an 'attractive rose pergola'; fancy coming close to divorce over an attractive rose pergola!

- the back garden, which has been an uncontrollable wilderness ever since you moved in, has been transformed into an 'attractive cottage-style garden'; and it is invariably 'laid to lawn': what 'laid to lawn' really means I have never been able to discover, but it sounds better than 'laid to weeds, moss, clover and bare patches';

- the peeling paintwork has suddenly become 'well presented and maintained': presumably this means well presented and maintained peeling;

- the pokey little kitchen has become 'a compact, efficient galley kitchen';

- the ghastly stone-effect fireplace in the sitting room which has been driving you to the point of psychiatric treatment for years has become 'a feature fireplace' (presumably because it came close to featuring largely in your imminent insanity);

- the strange tiles in the hallway, which you always presumed were a design fault, have been transformed into 'exclusive handmade de Vacchio tiling' (if only you'd known before you put the house on the market!);

- the wreck of a garden shed and lean-to coal house that you thought would reduce the value of the property by at least £5000 have become 'an extensive and flexible range of outbuildings' (flexible because they move every time the wind blows);

- the slum of an area in which the house was cursed to exist has suddenly become 'an increasingly popular area' (well, let's face it, it couldn't become *less* popular);

- the rooms into which you can scarcely fit any furniture become 'accommodation designed for easy management' (after all, if there's no furniture there, and you can't live in them, they are bound to be reasonably easy to manage).

Faced with this sort of enlightenment, it's a wonder the idea of moving to a new house ever entered your mind.

TYPES OF VIEWER

When you put your house on the market, you'll quickly come to discover that viewers fall into a number of distinct categories. The very worst type of viewer is the one who insists he can only manage to view during one particular hour at weekends and then turns up two hours late, with four unruly children, all in muddy shoes, a large dog, an aged aunt who gives the distinct impression of being doubly incontinent, and who then proceeds to take a whole hour wandering around your immaculately tidy abode, poking into every cupboard, leaving greasy fingermarks everywhere and spilling a cup of tea over the only decent carpet in the house; and then, on the way out, just after the dog has had an 'accident' in the hallway, turns to you and announces, 'It's not really what we were after, you know.' Not all viewers are this bad, of course; some leave the dog in the car.

The more important categories of viewer are described below.

- The it-was-a-mistake viewer: this is the one who reveals, as he or she goes around the house, that coming at all was a mistake. For example, he suddenly realizes the house is three-bedroomed whereas he wanted four, that the heating is oil-fired whereas they would only ever consider gas, that the house is in the town whereas they wanted to live in the country, that the house points west whereas they wanted one which points east, that the house is a semi whereas they wanted a detached – even though they knew all the facts from the estate agents' details.

- The environmentalist: this type of viewer shows an almost complete lack of interest in the house itself and simply bombards you with questions about the neighbours, the schools, how close the shops are, if the noise from the railway is bad at night, how long it takes to get to the M4, how high the rates are, when the bins are emptied and whether the road is 'maintained' or not. Why he bothers with a house at all is a mystery, when he could simply find the location that fits the bill and pitch a tent there.

- The it's-very-nice viewer: this type of viewer looks at the outside of the house and says 'very nice', peers into the sitting room and says, 'very nice', walks into the bathroom and declares 'very nice', as is the kitchen, the main bedroom, the airing cupboard, the fireplace, the light switches, the manhole cover outside, and even the tiles on the roof. In fact, mention to this type of viewer that the house has dry rot, deathwatch beetle, subsidence and rising damp, and the chances are they'll still say 'very nice'. One common feature of them all is that, having announced that everything in sight is 'very nice', they'll tell you as they leave that 'It's not quite what we want'.

- The planner: this type of vendor stalks quickly around the house uttering things like 'If we knock that wall down, bung in an RSJ, lower the floor six inches and re-align the partition wall then we'll be able to extend ourwards eight feet, incorporate a solar-heated indoor water garden and make room for our TV satellite dish on the roof.' In practice, once he moves in, he'll leave the house totally unaltered for 15 years whilst he revises and re-revises his plans.

- The middle-class trendy: the middle-class trendy viewer is a real inverted snob and will rave about items like outside toilets ('Terrific . . . we can rip out the low-level WC and restore the outside loo with a reproduction Thomas Crapper high-level bell-flush cistern with a long chain. How really super and artisan!'), open fires ('I don't want Toby and Jocasta to grow up with unhealthy positive-ion-laden centrally heated air'), backyards ('How delight-fully non-materialistic!') and grotty neighbourhoods ('I want Toby and Jocasta to mix with all classes of children'). In fact, all the features of the house which make *you* want to leave it are the very reasons why he or she considers it so desirable.

- The posers: they look disdainfully at your small, narrow drive and remark, 'Daddy will have trouble parking the Rolls when he comes to see us,' and one look at the dining room will produce the response, 'Well, we'd have to cut down on dinner-party guests, I suppose', promptly countered by 'Of course we weekend in the country most of the time', and a general comment on your choice of decoration will be rounded off by 'Quaint, but of course we'll be getting darling David Hicks to cast an eye over the decor.'

- The chatterboxes: by the time they have been in your house for half an hour you'll know their entire life story, the nature of the unpleasant operation she had last July, why they don't talk about Cousin Edith, where they are going for their summer holiday (you may even end up getting a postcard), how long it took Uncle Jim's colostomy to settle down, intimate details about their current neighbours and why they will be glad to move away from them, their shoe size, food preferences, choice of washing powder, how they voted at the last election, and so on.

- The silent viewer: he will walk round your house for up to an hour without uttering one single word. Indeed, in the most extreme cases, he'll walk in without even a 'Hello' or any indication about where he came from except for a wave of a sheet of estate agent's details. Normally the only verbal communication will be a cursory 'Very nice, but not for us' as he hurries down the drive, never to be seen again.

- The 'shame-about-the' viewer: his comments on the house are confined to 'Shame about the view', 'Shame about the garden', 'Shame about the carpets/chimney/roof/window-frames/neighbours' dog/smell/noise/price/area/ country/inflation rate/Soviet foreign policy', etc. In fact it is a shame about everything, including the fact that he ever stepped over the threshold.

- The viewing-for-a-friend viewer: this is an odd category which, for some strange reason, prefers to pretend he is not looking for himself (or herself) but for a friend or relative (a brother working in the Gulf is one of the commonest excuses).

WAYS OF DISCOURAGING POTENTIAL BUYERS YOU DON'T LIKE

Most people grow to love their house like a dear friend or relative, and forgive its shortcomings and weaknesses. And so, when the time comes to move, they are often reluctant to sell to someone they don't like; it would be rather like abandoning their own grandmother in her old age to a life of desperate exile. If this happens to you, it is vital that you have at your disposal some effective means for discouraging the unsuitable buyer. Listed below are some suitable phrases to drop into casual conversation with the buyer:

- 'I'm glad the public health inspector has at last allowed us to put the house on the market'

- 'We normally try to spread the load by sleeping in different rooms'

- 'Don't worry about the motorway interchange . . . it will be well clear of the flower borders'

- 'I'm so glad you came on a dry day'

- 'Don't go into the loft when there's a full moon'

- 'Don't listen to any silly stories about the radiation scare'

- 'I hope you manage to stay here longer than we could'

- 'It was such a relief to the building society when we put the house on the market'

- 'Just to be on the safe side, we had the cellar sealed up'

- 'The rats are good company most of the time'

- 'Would you mind if I showed you photos of the garden? It might be safer than going outside when the people next door are in'

- 'We normally sleep downstairs in windy weather'

- 'That surveyor you sent was the bravest man I've ever met'

- 'I hope you're not superstitious'

- 'It's wise to go away at weekends if the vicar's not around'

- 'The agent said you were broadminded'

- 'I hope the estate agent's details were OK . . . his doctor advised him against coming round in person'

- 'Don't worry . . . we've managed to get rid of most of the bloodstains.'

'If you're going to sell the house yourself you have to accept that some viewers won't be interested.'

HOW TO SELL YOUR HOUSE YOURSELF

Estate agents' fees are often one of the major costs involved in moving house. Typically you will be asked to pay 1 or 2 per cent of the sale price to the agent; if he manages to sell your house on the strength of one single phone call this may seem an excessive commission. Not surprisingly, many people try to economize on the total cost of moving by missing out the agent entirely and selling the house themselves. This may sound easy and tempting, especially if you have had bad experiences of agents in the past; but in practice it can be a lot more difficult than it sounds. Among the different ways of selling a house are:

- Put up a 'For Sale' sign outside your house. If your house faces a main road, or is on the hard shoulder of the M1, this can be effective as it will at least be seen by lots of people. If you live on the 20th floor of a tower block, then you are likely to attract only very tall purchasers.

- Put up a 'For Sale' sign inside your house. Although this may be somewhat less effective, and be seen by a rather restricted range of people, it does have the advantage that the sign lasts longer.

- Put a 'Not for Sale Under *any* Circumstances Whatsoever' sign outside your house, and wait for people's curiosity to get the better of them.

- Put an ad in the paper. The local paper is often the best bet, but *Country Life* or *The Field* may be better, although much more expensive, if you wish to attract the wealthier buyers. *Beano* is a lot cheaper, but attracts less affluent readers.

- Walk around with a sandwich board.

- Walk around with a sandwich; in practice this may be less productive than the sandwich board, but tastes better. Also you may find selling the sandwich (provided it is fresh) a lot easier than selling the house.

- Put an ad on TV. This is perhaps the flashiest method of selling, and probably the most expensive (in fact, having the ad ploughed into the lunar dust by a remote control moon buggy is more expensive, but reaches a smaller and more specialist audience and therefore is scarcely worth the extra).

- Have a pop-song written about your house. The main snag is that before it reaches the charts, and is hence heard by a sufficient number of people, you may have sold your house in the more conventional way.

- Shout 'For Sale!' loudly from the upstairs window. This is OK if you live in a town, but less effective on a remote Hebridean island. Also, make sure people realize it's the house that's for sale and not you, otherwise you may get some very strange (and probably disappointing) offers.

- Have 'For Sale' T-shirts printed and sold on Oxford Street. Definitely one of the trendier methods, but in practice less effective than more conventional means such as 'For Sale' ice creams and candy floss.

- Lobby your MP to bring a motion in Parliament making it compulsory for anyone over the age of 18 to put an offer on your house.

- Sell lottery tickets for your house. The snag is not knowing in advance the total proceeds from the lottery, and hence whether you will actually make a profit or not.

- Auction it yourself.

- Write 'For Sale' graffiti in the local public toilets. Cheap, but you may get a rather strange clientele.

- Employ a leading composer to write an opera about selling your house, and hire the Royal Opera House, Covent Garden to get it staged. This is selling a house in *real* style.

'Now, as you may have gathered, something went slightly wrong on exchange . . .'

ADDRESSES

When you come to sell a house, the address of the property can often be the most pertinent selling feature of all, so it must sound right. 'Sound' is the all-important word, because it is where the house sounds as though it is, rather than where it actually is, which matters. To an American, 135505B Pennsylvania Street West is a perfectly acceptable address, and without an intimate knowledge of the area you have no way of knowing whether the area is good or bad, or whether the house is a 12-bedroomed colonial mansion or a simple timber bungalow. Similarly in France 5225 Rue St Jacques could be anything from a simple terraced house to a Louis XIV urban château, whilst in Hong Kong an address such as Flat D, Block 14, 12th Floor, Ngai Chi Road could be a one-room resettlement flat for Vietnamese refugees or a £4 million penthouse with a breathtaking view over the harbour. In Britain, however:

- The house should have a name. All self-respecting houses have names, however meaningless they may be, and often are: for example, Four Oaks (where the only greenery is in a window-box), Fairlawns (where the only patch of grass was tarmacked 25 years ago), Dunroamin (where nobody has lived for more than two years at a stretch), Belle View (overlooking the sewage works), or Robin's Nest (whose owner, named Fred, hates birds). Giving a house a name suggests it is only a small step removed from a castle or manor house, and generally adds about £10,000 to the price that could otherwise be asked.

- Ideally the house should not have a number; numbers suggest large, anonymous estates, and row upon row of similarity. To the British house-owner, the house is his or her castle, and castles don't grow on estates. If, however, the house must have a numerical identity, the number must be small – ideally, less than 10. High numbers such as 256 suggest large estates, and the only thing worse is to have a number qualified by a letter; for example, was 124b built in an unwanted corner of the garden of 124, or is it the top-floor flat, or is it the pokey second half of what, even at its prime, was only a small detached dwelling? In all instances it is something to avoid like the plague.

- If the house has to have a number, avoid giving it a name as well, which would smack of a lower-class area: it suggests that the owners aspire to a house with a name but haven't quite made it yet. The sort of names found linked to numbers include Casa Nova, Belview, Torremolinos, Inglenook, Sunnycove, Camelot, etc. Almost all these will be dismissed summarily by the serious upwardly mobile house-buyer, and if you wish to catch this type of buyer the best thing to do is to drop the name completely and come clean with a simple number.

- There is a clear hierarchy for road names. Amongst the more acceptable are Grove, Avenue and Gardens; slightly less desirable are Road, Close and Lane; at the bottom of the heap are Street, Terrace, Alley and Buildings. A desirable detached, neo-Georgian, 5-bedroomed house lumbered with an address like 34b Tripe Alley, off Gas Works Street will fetch only half the price of a rotting timber shack which delights in the designation Rose Cottage, The Green.

- In some areas a certain degree of middle-class snobbery attaches to house names which suggest chic conversions from previously quaint but undesirable properties; so for example we see high prices asked for The Old Windmill, The Potteries, The Old Bakehouse, The Old Post House, The Maltings, etc. The magic word 'Old' in the name is always an advantage.

- Generally speaking, the shorter the address the better. Therefore 'Eastings, Maltby' is preferable to 'Wisteria Cottage, The Green, Arlingford Row, Cosingtree, Neasefield, Near Ousefield, Wokingford, Wiltshire'. The former suggests that everyone, just everyone, knows the property, whilst the latter indicates that only someone with an intimate knowledge of the area and a first-class honours degree in geography would find it first go.

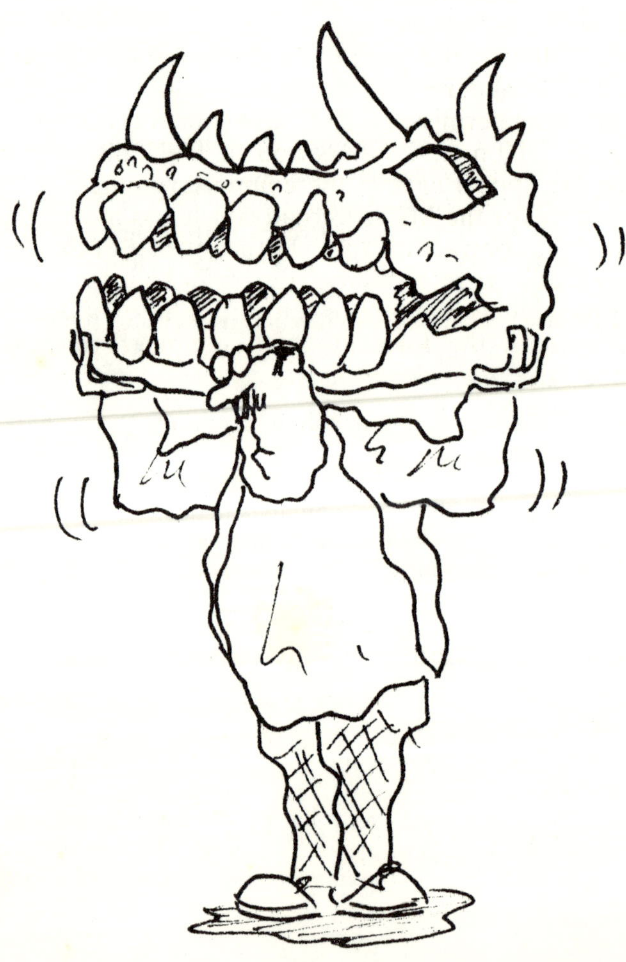

TECHNICAL PROBLEMS WITH MOVING HOUSE

Many technical problems can arise when you move house. These range from the trivial (such as finding that your old curtains clash with the next-door neighbour's wallpaper) to the serious (such as finding that the new house doesn't actually exist, but was purely a figment of the estate agent's imagination). Sometimes problems come singly, sometimes they come in bargain packs of two, three, four or more; for example, you discover the contract has got lost in the post, so you get the solicitor to prepare a new one, but the delay means you miss that month's mortgage allocation, so you re-submit the application to the building society, but then your buyer pulls out because he was impatient to move, and then, just as you find a new buyer, the surveyor's report on your house gets mixed up with one on the local derelict abattoir, local searches suggest that the house never had planning permission at all, and your solicitor gets arrested for his part in a gold-bullion raid; his period of bail fails to coincide with the deadline for the appeal against the compulsory purchase order placed on the new property for the M25 slip road which was moved from its previous route because the contractor, who was the brother of the derelict abattoir's owner's neighbour, went broke because your solicitor revealed during his committal proceedings that he was the very same contractor who built your new house without the formality of planning permission. Finally your appeal to the Pope for priority mortgage consideration gets turned down because the house isn't on main drainage, and this turns out to be contrary to local papal edicts. This sort of experience is far from rare when moving house.

Some of the serious snags you might encounter when you move are:

- the address on the contract is wrong;

- the house is listed as being of historical interest and must have repairs carried out without delay in order not to contravene regulations;

- the house is the subject of a compulsory purchase order;

- the house is in contravention of a Right of Ancient Lights;

- the colour scheme of the house's exterior is in contravention of the Geneva Convention on Human Rights;

- the house never had planning permission;

- the house had planning permission, but only as a maggot farm;

- the house turns out still to be functioning as a maggot farm;

- the internal decoration is a public joke, but the house has no licence for public entertainment;

- the person who gazumped you at the last minute turns out to be your solicitor;

- the house is in breach of a probation order (rare);

- the house is next door to that of your mother-in-law (try to think of a worse technical problem than this one);

- the house exists in an as-yet-undiscovered physical dimension, and is difficult for anyone who is less than a full professor of physics to find;

- the house has a sitting tenant;

- the house has a standing tenant (not quite as bad as a sitting tenant, as they leave more room for you to move around);

- the house is past its 'best before' date.

'Owing to a slight technical oversight, I've accidentally sold your house to myself for £1.25 . . . sorry.'

THE COST OF MOVING HOUSE

On the absolute scale of difficulty, underestimating the cost of moving house ranks, for easiness, somewhere between crushing a wilting daisy and picking your nose. In my own experience of moving, even if I've taken my most pessimistic estimate of the costs, doubled it, added £2000 and doubled it again, I have usually been 300 per cent out on the downside. Basically, moving house is a rich man's sport on a par with polo, ocean yacht-racing and race-horse breeding; unfortunately, whilst the costs are on a par with these exotic pastimes, the resultant pleasure is not. It is like polo without the ponies, ocean yacht-racing without the yacht, and race-horse breeding scaled down to the enjoyment quotient of farming fruit flies. This may sound cynical, but it is not that far removed from the truth.

Let us consider the costs involved. The average house-buyer will jot down the following major expenses when assessing whether he or she can actually afford to move:

solicitors' fees	£850
estate agent's fees	£200
cost of survey	£450
stamp duty	£1000
removal costs	£450
miscellaneous costs	£500

Total costs	**£5250**

Faced with these sorts of figures, most buyers decide that a move is probably worth while given that they'll stay in their new house for a good five or ten years. Over this period of time, a few thousand pounds soon pales to insignificance. Unfortunately, these simple sums, which we all carry out, miss out a large proportion of the real expenses involved. In practice the following items should be added to the shopping list:

- the hidden repairs which were not worthy of the surveyor's attention but on which the very future of your marriage depends £2000

- the cost of new curtains, because your old ones don't fit the windows in the new house £800

- the cost of new carpets, because the ones you bought for an arm and a leg from the vendor don't match the new curtains you bought £1500

- the cost of a new three-piece suite, because your old one now looks shabby beside the new carpets and new curtains £1500

- the cost of new bedclothes, because having spent so much on new carpets it seems a false economy not to get co-ordinating bed linen £300

- the cost of a new bathroom suite because, having now done so much to smarten up the rest of the house, the bathroom looks tatty £900

- the cost of new school uniforms for your children because they now live too far from their old school £300

- the cost of ferrying your children from the new house to the old area so that they can still play with their old friends (first five years' costs) £350

- the cost of a house-warming party £450

- the cost of replacing the sitting-room carpet after the house-warming party £800

- the cost of new clothes for the party £200

- the cost of entertaining the new neighbours to repay their generosity when you first moved in £300

- the cost of extra visits from friends and relatives to view your new house £250

- the cost of meals eaten out whilst settling in because the kitchen is unusable £120

- the cost of petrol for taking all the rubbish to the tip £50

- the cost of repairs to the car because you tried to carry too much rubbish £550

- the cost of a new car when you suddenly realize the old one looks tatty beside your neighbours' cars £8550

- the cost of clothes and toys to bring your children up to the standard of the neighbourhood £600

- the cost of a new bed so that you can spend the restless nights worrying about the cost of it all in comfort £250

- the cost of a complete new bedroom to match the new bed £2500

- the cost of mix-ups with standing orders, etc. £400

- the cost of not having a sufficiently good knowledge of local shops, and making abortive visits to buy various essential items £150

- the cost of various items of lost postage £80

- the cost of sacrificed career opportunities through resolving never to move again £25,000

- the cost of divorce proceedings when you don't get around to all the jobs you promised you would........................... £1500

- alimony (first 5 years).. £25,000

- cost of four weeks in a rest home getting over the divorce £2000

- the cost of the hair transplant required to give you any chance at all of ever finding a new spouse............................. £1500

- the insurance costs and lost earnings from the shortened life span resulting from the above..................................... £35,000

Total hidden costs   **£112,900**

================

In other words, the hidden costs of moving house amount to about £113,000. If you add on the obvious charges of about £5250 you end up with a cost of removal of over £118,000 . . . Draw your own conclusions as to whether it is worth it.

MOVING HOUSE AND SEX

There is really no legitimate connection at all between sex and moving house. However, having raised the subject if not the passions, it is worth while pondering on the main differences between sex and changing house:

- moving house normally takes between two and three months to complete: sex, on the other hand, is normally completed somewhat more quickly (except in the case of people with the most remarkable degree of self-control and lots of spare time, or people of very advanced age);

- moving house normally costs at least £4000: sex is usually a lot cheaper, probably as it does not normally need more than one man, and a large van is a non-essential luxury (if you find sex more expensive than this, then it might be worth while taking up moving house as a hobby in order to save money);

- most people move house two or three times in their life: except for the very unfortunate amongst us, sex usually takes place more often;

- when moving house, the bed invariably moves off the floor: the bed only moves off the floor during sex on those really special occasions;

- it can take months or even years to recover fully from moving house: in my experience the recovery time after sex is shorter;

- moving house needs the assistance of a solicitor: sex can benefit from the help of a solicitor, especially if he or she is especially athletic, but it is not essential;

- it is wise to have a house structurally surveyed before buying: it is not normally necessary to have your partner structurally surveyed before sex, even if he or she is advanced in years;

- most people borrow money from a bank or building society to buy a house: lenders normally take a less generous view towards raising a loan for sex;

- you can get tax relief on money borrowed for house purchase: I have yet to hear of anyone gaining tax relief on money spent on sex (if any readers know a way, please let the author know without delay, and certainly before 6 April next year);

- house purchase often starts in an estate agent's office: sex doesn't very often start there, although it is almost certain that estate agents would encourage it if they thought they could get some commission;

- you can't easily move house staying in bed;

- you normally move house fully-clothed: only people in a real hurry, the very shy or the excessively formal have sex fully clothed;

'There's been some misunderstanding . . . the £45,000 was just for the photograph.'

- you examine details of a house in full before viewing and entering: any request to examine the details of your partner before viewing and entering might hint of an excessively unromantic attitude to sex;

- sex only rarely results in searches at the Land Registry;

- after moving house successfully people often invite friends round for a drink to celebrate: after making love successfully it is not common to invite friends round to celebrate;

- house-moving reaches a climax on removal day: sex can reach a climax any day;

- both are concerned with erections of one sort or another, but in the case of house-moving the erections are usually more permanent;

- people moan at each other during sex: during house moves they usually moan at the removal men, solicitors and estate agents instead;

- house moves are normally based on a legal contract: this is rare in sex;

- house-buying requires witnesses when you sign the contract: sex does not require witnesses, but it can be quite exciting to have them sometimes;

- you normally get quotes from the different parties involved in house purchase, and often end up going to the cheapest: in the case of sex quotes are not normal, and in any case the cheapest may not be the best;

- it is difficult to move house on Sundays: I have found little problem with sex on the sabbath;

- you can insure against failure in moving house: Insurance companies are less understanding about failure in sex;

- the drawbacks to a new house can emerge at almost any time, even years later: the drawbacks of sex have a habit of emerging almost exactly 9 months later;

- the process of moving house is not exactly fun – you do it in order to live somewhere else: with sex the fun is in the doing rather than in the subsequent state.

FREQUENCY OF MOVING HOUSE

One of the questions people often ask themselves is how often they ought to move. This is, of course, a complex question depending upon personal circumstances, income, tax position, whether they are wanted by the police, and so on. Sometimes, because of job commitments, the question is academic, but if you do have a choice the following factors are worth considering in relation to the elapsed time between moves:

every 100 years	Not very exciting as a way of life. You have to be pretty confident that the house you have chosen is the right one for you. Also, if you live to be over 120 you might find the disruption of moving a little too much at that time of life.
every 30 years	This means that most people would move only once. It does have the advantage that you'll only suffer estate agents once, but the scope for moving up-market is limited.
every 10 years	Gives a bit more variety to life, but you might still get a bit stale in each house.
every 5 years	About ideal from most points of view. Allows you to experience a variety of houses, to move up-market a bit, as well as to recover from the considerable cost of removal each time.
every year	Too frequent from a financial point of view; you won't easily recover the removal costs unless you can be sure the property's value will increase substantially within twelve months.
every month	As many bills are sent out monthly, you could escape in time before having to pay most of them. But the bills would have to be really big to compensate for the removal costs. You might also escape ever actually making a mortgage repayment, but you are likely to exhaust possible sources of finance fairly quickly. If however you wish to avoid certain people, such as your mother-in-law, moving monthly could be a wise strategy.
every week	Whilst expensive, you can at least save on housework and gardening if you choose your new house carefully (i.e. always move to houses where the vacuuming has been done and the grass is short). Also allows you considerable variety, in that you stand a chance of experiencing up to 4000 different houses over 40 years (albeit at a cost of about £8,000,000 in estate agent's fees . . . indeed it would be cheaper to take over a substantial estate agency just to handle your transactions). You might have to allow up to two days each week to

hunt for a new house to move to, and this could become
increasingly difficult after the first few years.

every day

This maximizes the variety, and would allow you to live in
about 10 per cent of all the houses in the British Isles at some
time. Great for house-fetishists, and you need never do any
cleaning, and are unlikely to be caught up by any bills. The
drawback is that you'll end up spending most of your life in
removal vans, and are unlikely to make any new friends
outside the rather limited fields of removal companies, the
faster-working solicitors, and estate agents. Also it will be a
matter of house-hunting in the morning, moving in the
afternoon, and showing prospective buyers around in the
evening. Unless you wish to treat moving as your only
hobby, try a more settled pattern of life.

*'Congratulations . . . none of us at Taylor, Wilkins & Partners thought you'd
last out the first month at no. 8, after all the gruesome stories we'd heard!'*

A FINAL WORD

Once I'd finished the manuscript of this book, I sat back and started to worry about what I'd written. Would I put people off moving house? Had I painted too gloomy a picture of the problems? I read the manuscript again and again, and asked myself the following searching questions:

- Had I been a little too hard on estate agents? After all, my Great Aunt Maud once met someone whilst on holiday in Bognor who had once lived next door to someone whose cousin nearly married a man whose father once sold a car to the friend of a chap who knew an estate agent who was almost decent and honest. Maybe there are others like him.

- Had I over-stated the amount of money solicitors charge for signing a few letters and sticking a few stamps on envelopes? After all, I did hear of a lady who had an affair with the brother of the friend of a solicitor who was so poor that he once had to cancel his annual holiday in Barbados because he couldn't otherwise afford to get his Rolls serviced.

- Did I give the impression that *all* surveyors' reports are impossible to understand? I must confess that when I first bought a house the surveyor's report was actually quite easy to understand (mind you, all it said was 'Don't under any circumstances buy this laughable imitation of a dwelling').

- Had I made readers fear that *all* houses are riddled with woodworm, dry rot, subsidence and deathwatch beetle? After all, I do know of a little semi in Watford which manages to scrape by with only rising damp and woodworm, although it is not on the market.

- Had I over-stated the amount of mind-rotting disruption caused by moving house? After all, I did once meet someone who had moved at least three times in his life and never spent more than six weeks in a state of total mental collapse.

- Had I over-estimated the total cost of moving, and the dire poverty which reigns afterwards? To be honest, last time we moved it was only two years before we'd managed to scrape enough savings together to go out for a meal (although it was only to a Wimpy bar), so it can't be all that bad.

As I sat there in the chaos of my study, still packed to the ceiling in cardboard boxes from our last move two years ago, on the rickety chair which I would have repaired months ago if I'd had the money, living in fear of ever hearing the words 'estate agent' again lest I revert to the condition of mental jelly I remembered so well, I read the manuscript again and passed a final judgement on the contents. Had I spread excessive gloom and despondency over moving house?

The answer was perfectly clear. No, I hadn't.

GAZUMPED
FOR
SALE
SOLD